A LITTLE GUIDE TO TREES

CHARLOTTE VOAKE

Text by Kate Petty and Jo Elworthy

EDEN PROJECT
BOOKS

CONTENTS

INTRODUCTION

Discover the names of the trees you see all around you: in the town and in the country, in your garden and in the woods, by the roadsides and riversides and in the park.

In this book you'll find clues to help you work out which tree is which. Look out for the tree's shape and size and where you find it growing. Look at the shapes of the leaves. On some pages you'll find drawings of the buds in winter so you can still name your tree even when the leaves have fallen off.

Remember, don't eat any leaves or fruits unless an adult who knows what's what says it's OK. And always take the book to the tree rather than the tree to the book!

WHAT ARE TREES?

These green giants are the biggest plants on Earth. Many have been around for centuries, some since the age of dinosaurs.

Trees have strong trunks which hold up branches and twigs covered in leaves. Leaves are like little factories! They absorb sunshine and carbon dioxide gas from the air and water from the ground turning these ingredients into 'tree food' for energy and growth. This process also makes oxygen which they breathe out for us to breathe in! Trees produce water vapour to help make clouds and rain, and provide shade, shelter and timber.

Hurrah for trees!

SEASONS

Trees will look different depending on what season of the year you see them in.

SPRING

Most trees you see will be full of flowers in the early months of the year. Many trees have male and female flowers. On some trees these grow together; on others they grow on different trees.

SUMMER

This is the best time to identify a tree by its leaves. There are so many different shapes!

AUTUMN

Autumn brings a burst of colour! The leaves of some trees turn from green to yellow to red to golden brown, before falling to the ground.

WINTER

Deciduous trees drop their leaves every winter and go to sleep, waiting for spring. Evergreen trees keep their leaves all year round.

GROW YOUR OWN TREE

Growing your own tree can be fun!
Start looking for seeds in the autumn.
Some easy ones to spot are acorns or conkers.

What you'll need: a flowerpot for each seed,
some garden soil and some labels

1. Collect your seeds.
2. Fill each flowerpot
with soil and bury
the seeds so they are
just covered.
3. Label each pot.

Next spring you should see lots of
little seedlings growing in your pots.

Trees also replant themselves naturally. Depending on
the tree, the wind or a particular insect will carry the
pollen from the male to the female flower to make
a seed ~ a nut, a fruit, or a seed that looks like like a
toy helicopter. Each type of tree is different! When the
seed is ripe and it lands on the soil a new tree will start
to grow . . . and grow and grow!

6

HOW TO
MEASURE
A TREE

Find a friend, a tree, a pencil or stick
and a tape measure.

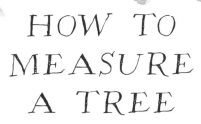

1. Get your friend
to wait by the tree while
you walk away. Stand far
enough away so that you
can see the whole tree.

2. CLOSE ONE EYE.
Hold your pencil at arm's
length in front of you
until it looks as if it is
the same height as
the tree.

3. Keep the bottom of
the pencil in line with
the bottom of the tree
and turn the 'top end'
downwards so it's
parallel with the
ground.

4. Now, get your friend to
run along the ground to the spot
at the very tip of the pencil ~
KEEP ONE EYE CLOSED!

5. Now measure the distance
between your friend and the tree.
That measurement is the
height of the tree.

BEECH

Fagus sylvatica
Beech family
Up to 40m
Deciduous

THE BARK OF THE BEECH IS VERY SMOOTH, SO IF YOU FIND A TREE WITH SOMEONE'S INITIALS CUT INTO IT, IT MAY WELL BE A BEECH.

This towering tree has grey bark and bright green leaves. The ground beneath is often bare except for dead beech leaves and seed cases (masts) so it is easy to see an old tree's gnarled roots.

IN SPRING

The new leaves are delicate
and soft with a slight shine.

IN AUTUMN

The leaves turn a rusty brown.
Beech nuts grow
in small prickly
cases called masts.

BEECH

IN WINTER

Deer, badgers,
squirrels, mice
and birds ~ like
the brambling
and chaffinch ~
love to feast on
beech nuts.

CATERPILLARS OF THE LOBSTER MOTH FEED ON BEECH LEAVES.

Winter
buds are
slim and
pointed.

For centuries pigs have been let into beech woods to eat the nuts.

Bare
branches
end in
twigs
which
look like
feathers
against
the sky.

HORNBEAM

Carpinus betulus
Birch family
Up to 30m
Deciduous

The hornbeam has a bold outline with densely packed twigs and silver bark.

It is sometimes confused with the beech tree but hornbeam leaves have jagged edges and beech leaves have smooth edges.

IN SPRING

Look out for male catkins which are yellowy~green with red outer scales.

HORNBEAM

IN SUMMER

The leaves are oval and pointed with a rounded base and toothed edges.

IN AUTUMN

The leaves turn from green to yellow to orange to russet~brown. The fruits are called winged nutlets.

Hornbeam wood is very hard and heavy. It was used for piano hammers, wheel hubs, cogs for machinery, and butchers' blocks.

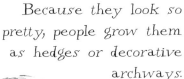

IN WINTER

WE HAWFINCHES ARE THE ONLY BIRDS WHICH CAN CRACK OPEN THE TOUGH SEEDS.

When hornbeams are planted in hedgerows they often keep their leaves right into the cold winter months. Their catkins are protected in buds from the cold winter weather.

Because they look so pretty, people grow them as hedges or decorative archways.

ALDER

Alnus glutinosa
Birch family
Up to 25m
Deciduous

Spot this
elegant domed
tree, with
its rounded
leaves
and reddish
branches,
on river banks.
Its roots
protect the
bank from
washing
away
and
provide a
home for
many animals.

I'M AN
ALDER KITTEN
MOTH
CATERPILLAR.

I'M AN
ALDER KITTEN
MOTH.

IN SPRING

Look out
for long
male catkins
which
release
clouds of pollen
in the spring,
and tiny female
cones which turn
from purple to green.

IN SUMMER

The leaves are dark green with little notches along the side and at the tip.

ALDER

ALDER WOOD HARDENS IN WATER, WHICH IS WHY IT IS SOMETIMES USED TO MAKE LOCK GATES IN CANALS.

In winter redpolls and siskins love eating the seeds found in the female cones.

IN AUTUMN

It's great to gather fallen brown cones and make your own miniature forests with them.

IN WINTER

The tiny winged seeds float like little boats in the water, so they can sail off and grow into trees far away.

Alder is often used to make clogs.

SILVER BIRCH

Betula pendula
Birch family
Up to 26m
Deciduous

This fast-growing, graceful tree is sometimes called 'the Lady of the Woods'. It is easy to spot with its white bark and pale green leaves. Compared to many other trees, the silver birch does not live a long time. It is often gone before 100 years have passed.

IN SUMMER

Leaves are delicate and fairly small with very pointy, toothed edges.

Birch twigs make great broomsticks.

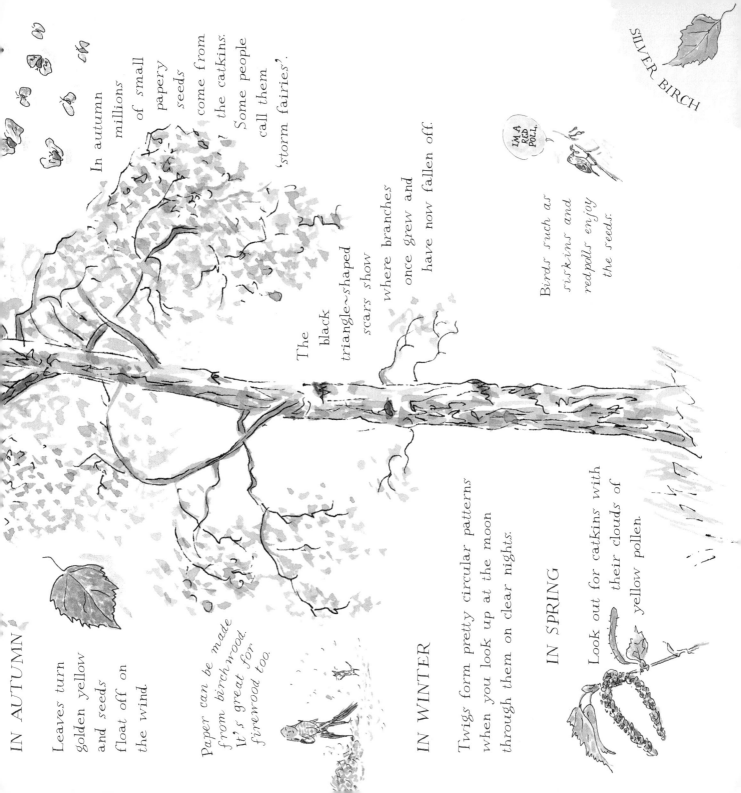

SILVER BIRCH

In autumn millions of small papery seeds come from the catkins. Some people call them 'storm fairies'.

The black triangle~shaped scars show where branches once grew and have now fallen off.

I'M A RED POLL.

Birds such as siskins and redpolls enjoy the seeds.

IN AUTUMN

Leaves turn golden yellow and seeds float off on the wind.

Paper can be made from birchwood. It's great for firewood too.

IN WINTER

Twigs form pretty circular patterns when you look up at the moon through them on clear nights.

IN SPRING

Look out for catkins with their clouds of yellow pollen.

LIME

Tilia cordata
Lime family
Up to 40m
Deciduous

NOT THIS KIND OF LIME.

You can *hear* this noisy tree from far away in summer as thousands of bees buzz round the blossoms. In prehistoric times it was one of our commonest trees. Its smooth grey bark gets rougher with age. Despite its name, green citrus lime fruits come from another sort of tree.

The lime is a tall column shape.

SOOTHING TEA IS MADE FROM LIME TREE FLOWERS. IT'S CALLED TILLEUL.

IN SPRING

The heart~shaped leaves have saw~toothed edges. Aphids like sucking the sap of the lime tree, which makes the tree and anything underneath it sticky with honeydew.

LIME

SLURP! SLURP!

Bzzzz

Bzzzzz

Bzzzzz

People carve beautiful things out of lime wood. These carvings can be found in St Paul's Cathedral in London.

IN SUMMER

The flowers hang from bracts, which look like leaves, and act as sails to carry the ripe fruits off on the wind.

Fashionable lime~tree avenues planted 400~500 years ago can still be seen today.

IN WINTER

Look for a tall trunk with upward~ pointing branches. Suckers round the trunk of the common lime make it look hairy.

You can tell limes by their whiskers and branches shaped like elbows!

17

WYCH ELM

Ulmus glabra
Elm family
Various, some up to 40m
Deciduous

Find this large,
stately tree growing
in damp places in woods,
near the sea and on
mountain slopes.

WYCH ELM

IN SPRING

The tiny female flowers open in early spring. These grow into papery green seeds after they have been pollinated.

The lop~sided leaves are oval shaped. Touch them gently. The upper surface is hairy and the lower surface soft.

THIS TREE LOVES DAMP PLACES.

HI! I'M AN ELM BARK BEETLE.

The wych elm is related to the English elm, which almost died out in the UK because of Dutch elm disease. This was caused by a fungus carried from tree to tree by elm bark beetles.

IN WINTER

Look out for the reddish~ brown, hairy buds.

IN SUMMER

Watch the seeds ripen to pale brown in July and fall from the tree.

LOMBARDY POPLAR

Populus nigra 'Italica'
Willow family
Up to 36m
Deciduous

Find this tall, elegant tree lining roadsides and in gardens throughout Europe. It originally came from Italy.

IN SPRING

Look out for bright red catkins, which are sometimes called 'devil's fingers'.

The white poplar is a close relative. The leaves are very pale underneath, and when the wind catches them, the whole tree can suddenly look white!

Wooden toys are often made from poplar timber as it does not splinter very easily.

I'M A POPLAR HAWK MOTH! SPOT ME NEAR THIS TREE.

LOMBARDY POPLAR

The branches often grow near the base.

Fruit punnets were once made from poplar wood.

IN AUTUMN

The glossy green leaves turn yellow.

ORCHARD

Orchards are gardens filled with fruit trees. In spring, they are like surprise weddings with trees wreathed in starry pink and white blossoms. Look closely ～ the flowers all look like little roses.

APRICOT

Prunus armeniaca
Rose family
Up to 4 m
Deciduous

PEAR

Pyrus communis
Rose family
Up to 4 m
Deciduous

Look out for white blossoms which are sometimes tinted yellow or pink.

Pear～tree flowers symbolize comfort and affection.

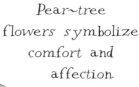

pear

Apricot trees have heart~shaped leaves and pretty pink blossoms.

CHERRY

Prunus avium
Rose family
Up to 15 m
Deciduous

The bark on the trunk is smooth and purplish~brown.

Cherry and plum blossoms celebrate the arrival of spring; they are the first trees in the orchard to flower.

APPLE

Malus domestica
Rose family
Up to 4 m
Deciduous

Apple blossoms are large and white with a pink tinge at the edges. The underside of their oval leaves is slightly furry.

plum

PLUM

Prunus domestica
Rose family
Up to 4 m
Deciduous

The bit in the middle of the plum blossom will grow into a fruit after it has been pollinated.

plum

Orchards in summer are buzzing with life. Bees carry pollen from flower to flower; the pollinated blossoms will soon grow into tasty fruits. Cherries first, then plums and, as summer turns to autumn, apples and pears ripen, ready to be picked!

PEAR

Fruits are delicious in jam and jellies but also straight off the tree. Pick pears when they are firm and let them ripen in the fruit bowl till they're sweet and juicy.

Fresh pears from the market at the end of the summer holidays are deliciously juicy and sweet.

APRICOT

Apricots originally came from China; now they are grown all over the world in places which have long, warm summers.

Apricots taste good dried or in jams.

CHERRY

Cherries can vary in colour from white to black to red.

Cherry wood makes great musical instruments.

24

Folklore says that if you hang all your old buckets in your plum tree it will bear more fruit.

PLUM

How many different sorts of plum can you find in the shops? They come in lots of different colours, from yellow to red to purplish blue.

APPLE

There are over 7,000 different sorts of apple ~ Cox, Bramley, Granny Smith, Discovery, Jupiter and Gala . . . Which ones have you tried?

Since Neolithic times apples have been grown for food, drink and medicine.

AN APPLE A DAY KEEPS THE DOCTOR AWAY!

Cows can get tipsy from eating windfall apples.

WILLOW

Salix spp
Willow family
Various, some up to 25m
Deciduous

THIS IS A CRACK WILLOW.

There are many sorts of willow. Most of them have long, thin leaves which are shiny and flutter in the slightest breeze. They have beautiful silky catkins called *pussy willows*. You will often find them growing near water.

weeping willow

HOWZAT!

The crack willow is common along the banks of rivers. The branches are brittle and, when they break, get carried along in the water. If they are washed against the bank they often take root and grow into a new crack willow.

The wood of the white willow is used to make cricket bats.

Weeping willows growing on dry land are great to make dens inside. Grow a living den simply by pushing long thin branches into the ground.

Willow stems can be woven into baskets and chairs.

OAK

Quercus spp
Beech family
Up to 30m
Deciduous

Summer leaves are dense and shady.

The mighty oak can live for over 700 years. You can recognize it straightaway by its sturdy shape, its zig zaggy branches and distinctive leaf shape.

IN SPRING

The little male flowers of oaks are called catkins. Early leaves are a brownish green.

People used to be married under oak trees.

In Sherwood Forest, Nottingham, stands the Major Oak, the largest oak tree in Britain. Robin Hood was said to have hidden in a big hollow tree trunk like this one.

sessile oak

IN AUTUMN

Find acorns scattered on the ground under oaks. The acorns from the English oak hang from stems; the acorns from the sessile oak have no stems. Plant some acorns and start your own oak forest!

OAK

English oak

Look out for 'knopper galls.' Gall wasp grubs have been laid inside!

In the past, ships were built from oak. It's still used to make furniture.

IN WINTER

Look for a tree with lots of twigs at the ends of crooked branches.

The evergreen holm oak, or holly oak, has shiny, leathery leaves all year round.

Gardeners plant scarlet oaks for their autumn colour.

SYCAMORE

Acer pseudoplatanus
Maple family
Up to 35m
Deciduous

Big, fast-growing sycamores have been around since medieval times and grow everywhere. You can spot them easily by their maple-shaped leaves and seeds that look like bunches of keys.

IN SPRING

Bright yellow flowers and green leaves arrive together.

WE ARE SYCAMORE MOTH CATERPILLARS.

AND WE LOVE TO EAT LEAVES, ESPECIALLY SYCAMORE ONES! YUM!

SYCAMORE

IN SUMMER

Listen out for the loud humming of busy bees as they collect nectar from the sycamore flowers.

IN AUTUMN

Tar-spot fungus attacks the leaves in autumn. It means they rot nice and quickly.

When the seeds turn brown they spin like little helicopters to the ground and quickly take root.

VIOLINS ARE OFTEN MADE FROM SYCAMORE WOOD.

SO ARE FLOORS.

IN WINTER

Look for tall, knobbly trunks with twigs clustered at the ends of crooked branches.

LONDON PLANE

*Platanus x hispanica
(x acerifolia)*
Plane family
Up to 44 m
Deciduous

Look out for this tree in towns and cities with its tall, tall trunk, spreading crown and tangly, twisty branches.

The bark on older trees peels off in patches so look out for mottled trunks. When it's really old it gets dark and cracked.

THE BARK LOOKS LIKE MY TROUSERS.

Developing fruits start off green then turn brown as they ripen.

IN SUMMER

Look out for the prickly, dangly, round fruits, which look like hundreds of fun earrings!

LOOK AT MY EARRINGS!

IN SPRING

The plane has huge leaves which are shaped like an open hand.

IN WINTER

The ripe brown fruits hang on the tree for many months after the leaves have fallen. The fruits break up, slowly releasing tiny seeds. The prickly hairs help carry the seeds away on the wind.

THIS MOTH EATS PLANE LEAVES.

Plane trees are very good at dealing with pollution and so are well~suited to living in cities around the world.

HORSE CHESTNUT

Aesculus
hippocastanum
Buckeye family
Up to 40m
Deciduous

Creamy, candle~like
flowers make this tree
easy to spot in May.
Gathering gleaming
conkers in their spiky
cases is fun in September.
The horse chestnut
originally came from the
Balkans. It isn't related to
the sweet chestnut.

Playing Conkers

Make a hole through a
conker. Thread a piece of
string through and knot the
end. Take turns to whack
the other person's conker.
If you break it, you are
the 'conqueror'!

IN SPRING

Look closely at a flower ~ it's pink and yellow as well as white.

HORSE CHESTNUT

The leaves open out like little umbrellas.

IN SUMMER

The leaves can grow as big as a grown~up's hand, sometimes bigger!

IN AUTUMN

The seeds of the horse chestnut are called conkers. They grow inside spiky green fruits which fall to the ground as they ripen, and split open. These conkers will grow into new trees.

Spiky fruit

Ripening fruit

Conker

I'M A LEAF MINING MOTH. MY CATERPILLARS MAKE TUNNELS IN THE LEAVES, MAKING THEM GO BLOTCHY.

IN WINTER

This tree is called 'horse chestnut' because of the horseshoe~ shaped scars left when the leaves drop off. Look out for big sticky buds and the flaky bark.

SWEET CHESTNUT

Castanea sativa
Beech family
Up to 35m
Deciduous

These lovely big trees have long handsome leaves, edible nuts and can live for over 500 years. Brought to Britain by the Romans, they grow naturally in sunny Italy and France.

CHESTNUTS ARE GOOD TO EAT! YUM!

36

IN SPRING and SUMMER

The leaves are large and spiky with pointed teeth on each leaf edge. They are glossy and quite leathery to the touch. Flowers appear in June and July.

IN AUTUMN

The leaves go a beautiful golden~yellow.

SWEET CHESTNUT

Hedgehog~like seed cases split open to reveal shiny, brown~skinned nuts. When cooked these are delicious.

All sorts of delicious cakes and puddings can be made out of sweetened chestnut purée.

IN WINTER

Once the leaves have fallen, it's easier to see how the bark grows in spiral ridges around the trunk.

The wood is very strong and can be made into fence posts.

ASH

Fraxinus excelsior
Olive family
Up to 40m
Deciduous

Look out for this tall graceful tree with its ash~grey trunk and upward~pointing branches. The fluttering circles of leaves are beautiful against a blue sky.

IN SPRING

Ash flowers between April and May. Look for velvety black buds and purply~yellow flowers.

Ash trees' deep roots take the goodness from the soil, so not much grows underneath them.

NOT MANY INSECTS LIVE IN ASH TREES SO YOU WON'T SEE MANY BIRDS...

BUT YOU MAY SPOT THE OCCASIONAL BLACKBIRD, CHAFFINCH, WREN OR ROBIN.

A tall trunk makes the ash hard to climb.

MMM~DELICIOUS LEAVES BUT BAD FOR MY BUTTER!

Ash wood is good for
furniture, carts and tool
handles because
its springiness makes
it a good shock absorber.

ASH

IN SUMMER

Ash leaflets grow
in pairs up the leaf
stalk with one
leaflet on
its own at
the end.

IN AUTUMN

Each seed is contained
in a twisted 'key' that
spins as it falls.

Ash trees live
for around
200 years. They
don't produce
seeds until they
are around
forty years old!

IN WINTER

Look out for grey twigs
with black buds coming
through.

Branches
curve down
and up
again, like
a candelabra.
Some brown
keys hang on.

39

ROWAN

Sorbus aucuparia
Rose family
Up to 20m
Deciduous

This pretty, slender tree is also called mountain ash. It has silvery bark and little leaves arranged like feathers.

In Greek legend, Zeus' eagle is said to have fought a demon to retrieve a stolen cup. Drops of its blood and feathers fell on the ground and grew into rowan trees. Its blood is the berries; its feathers are the leaves.

WE'RE HAPPY TO EAT THE BARK, TWIGS...

AND BERRIES TOO!

LOOK AT THE BOTTOM OF A ROWAN BERRY AND YOU WILL SEE A FIVE-POINTED STAR.

IN SPRING

Before the leaves appear look out for the young hairy twigs tinged with purple.

IN SUMMER

Clusters of creamy white flowers appear in May and June. Their strong, sweet smell attracts flies and beetles.

IN AUTUMN

Spot this tree in autumn and early winter when the bunches of red berries cling to the branches long after the leaves have fallen.

IN WINTER

Blackbirds and bullfinches feast on the berries. They are also an important winter food for the migratory birds such as redwings, fieldfares and waxwings.

Rowan takes its Latin name 'aucuparia' from the Latin word 'auceps', which means bird~catcher.

During the last century, bird~catchers in France and Germany used the berries in their traps to catch fieldfares and thrushes.

HEDGEROW

Hedgerows are the living boundaries that divide up our land.
If you look very closely, you'll see them bursting with life!
Birds, moths, butterflies, bats and dormice live and
feed inside their leafy walls.
In spring you'll find early primroses
sheltering beneath their skirts;
in summer they erupt in colourful
flowers. The autumn months bring
tasty nuts and berries whilst leafless
hedges in winter give refuge to slumbering animals.

Look out for these trees
growing in bushy
hedgerows:

Hazel

Field maple

Dog rose

Hawthorn

Blackthorn

Elder

HAZEL

Corylus avellana
Hazel family
4 to 7m
Deciduous

IN SPRING

Spot the dangly, yellow male flowers, called catkins or lamb's tails, and tiny red, spiky female flowers.

IN SUMMER

The leaves are rounded and soft with a pointed tip.

IN AUTUMN

Find tasty nuts for squirrels, nuthatches and you!

IN WINTER

See the light-coloured bark and oval, smooth buds on hairy twigs.

FIELD MAPLE

Acer campestre
Maple family
26m
Deciduous

ALL MAPLES HAVE A SUGARY SAP ESPECIALLY THE AMERICAN SUGAR MAPLE, WHICH MAPLE SYRUP IS MADE FROM.

IN SPRING

New leaves have a pinkish tinge.

IN SUMMER

The distinctively shaped leaves start to turn leathery and dark green.

IN AUTUMN

Watch the leaves turn bright yellow then reddish brown.

IN WINTER

Wood mice and bank voles love to eat the fallen seeds.

43

DOG ROSE

Rosa canina
Rose family
1 to 5m
Deciduous

IN SPRING

Stems grow
like spiky
green snakes
through bushes
and trees.

IN SUMMER

Find the
beautiful pale
pink flowers.

IN AUTUMN

Pick the rose hips for
making jelly but don't
eat them raw!

IN WINTER

Birds feast on the
tasty hips long into
the winter
months.

HAWTHORN

Crataegus monogyna
Rose family
7 to 10m
Deciduous

IN SPRING

The pale green leaves
are usually the
first to appear in
hedgerows. Spot the
white blossom in May.

IN SUMMER

Leaves
are small
and lobed.

IN AUTUMN

The red haws are a
tasty treat for thrushes
and waxwings.

IN WINTER

Look for bright red haws
clinging to silvery branches.

HAWTHORN
IS ALSO CALLED
THE FAIRY THORN.

BLACKTHORN

Prunus spinosa
Rose family
Up to 4 m
Deciduous

IN SPRING

Find the white blossoms on dark black bark. These appear even before the leaves.

IN SUMMER

Leaves are simply shaped and dull green in colour.

IN AUTUMN

Pick purple sloes for gin and jam. Be warned, they're sour if you eat them raw!

CHEERS!

IN WINTER

Look out for crooked branches and prickly thorns.

ELDER

Sambucus nigra
Honeysuckle family
3 to 10 m
Deciduous

IN SPRING

Umbrella~shaped flowers have a sickly sweet scent.

IN SUMMER

Light green leaves are made up of three to seven little leaflets.

IN AUTUMN

Clusters of black shiny berries can be made into wine. DON'T EAT THEM raw! They're very poisonous.

IN WINTER

Wintery stems often have a strange earlike fungus on them.

COMMON LARCH

Larix decidua
Pine family
Up to 35m
Deciduous

This tall tree often has a pointy tip and graceful, sweeping branches. Unlike other conifers, it drops its leaves in winter. It comes from the mountains of central and eastern Europe.

IN SPRING

Look out for the soft, pale green needle~like leaves. They grow in bunches of about forty. Spot the little red female cones and the golden~yellow male cones.

The bark is used to tan leather, making it strong, supple and long~lasting.

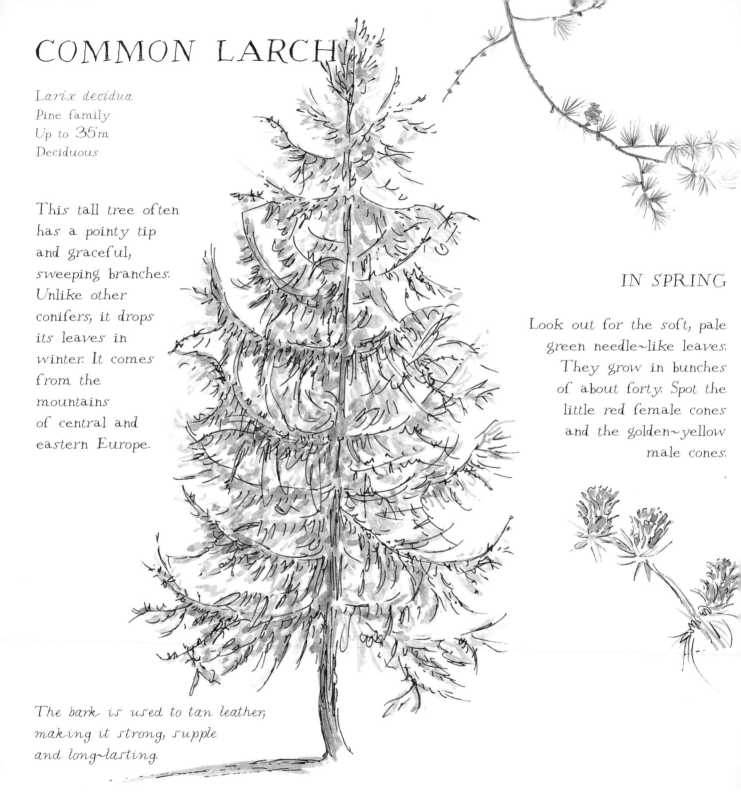

This is a little larch case-bearer moth. Its larvae eats larch needles. When there are lots of them, whole trees can get damaged.

The common crossbill eats the seeds. Its beak is specially shaped to get between the cone scales to get the seeds out.

IN AUTUMN

The needles change from light green to dark green with pale bands, to red, before finally turning yellow and dropping to the ground.

THE TIMBER IS USED TO MAKE FENCES, GATES AND GARDEN FURNITURE.

IN WINTER

In the coldest months look out for graceful sweeping branches which curve down, then up at the tips. You can also spot the ripe cones still clinging to the tree.

47

SCOTS PINE

Pinus sylvestris
Pine family
Up to 36m
Evergreen

An ancient
pine survivor from
the Ice Age, it is easy
to spot by its bare,
rusty~red trunk and
blue~green needles.

IN SPRING

In May, male
flowers have yellow
pollen and female flowers
are little pine cones
at the tips of
shoots.

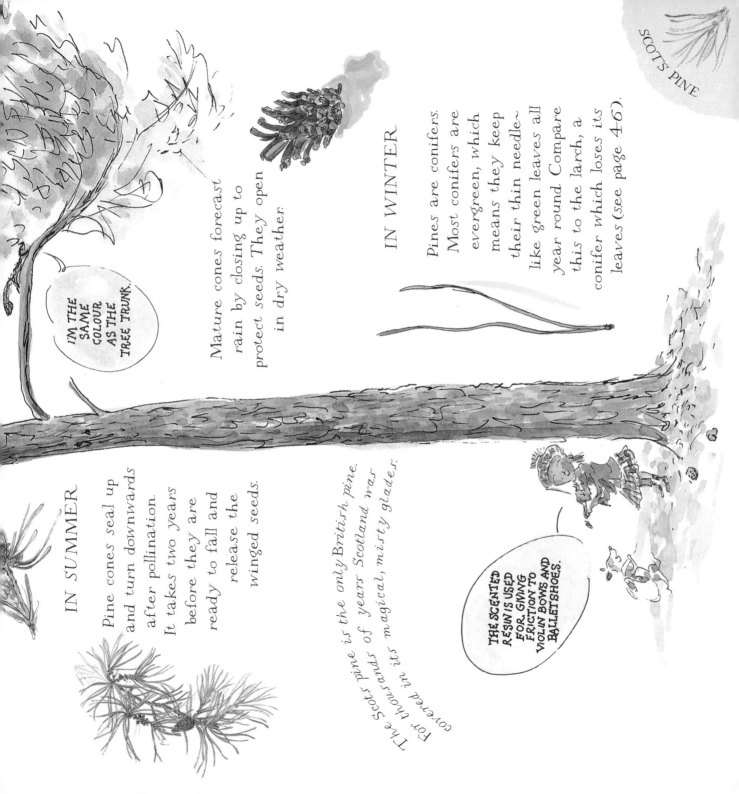

I'M THE SAME COLOUR AS THE TREE TRUNK.

Mature cones forecast rain by closing up to protect seeds. They open in dry weather.

IN WINTER

Pines are conifers. Most conifers are evergreen, which means they keep their thin needle-like green leaves all year round. Compare this to the larch, a conifer which loses its leaves (see page 46).

IN SUMMER

Pine cones seal up and turn downwards after pollination. It takes two years before they are ready to fall and release the winged seeds.

The Scots pine is the only British pine. For thousands of years Scotland was covered in its magical, misty glades.

THE SCENTED RESIN IS USED FOR GIVING FRICTION TO VIOLIN BOWS AND BALLET SHOES.

CEDAR OF LEBANON

Cedrus libani
Pine family
Up to 40m
Evergreen

A real giant,
this beautiful
tree has
branches
which spread out
sideways like
huge green plates.

Cedar timber was used to build ships over 4,000 years ago.

Cedars are evergreen and have needle~like leaves all year round. Cedars come from the mountain forests of Lebanon, Syria and southern Anatolia. People thought the tree was so beautiful that it has been planted in parks and gardens across the world.

The tree is the national emblem of Lebanon and can be seen on the Lebanese flag.

Cones take twelve months to develop and often grow every other year. They ripen from purplish~green to brown.

PEOPLE ONCE PUT THEIR CLOTHES IN CEDAR CHESTS TO WARD OFF THE MOTHS THAT EAT YOUR JUMPERS.

When the cones are ripe they break up to release winged seeds which are carried off by the wind.

The ancient Egyptians used this tree's resin to preserve mummies.

51

NORWAY SPRUCE

Picea abies
Pine family
Up to 44m
Evergreen

GOLDCRESTS LIKE TO SHELTER AND FEED IN THE BRANCHES.

Spot this tree on European mountains or in homes at Christmas time.

Legends say that a thousand years ago in Germany, St Boniface cut down an oak tree under which pagans were worshipping. A tree that looked like the Christmas trees we find today grew in its place and this was made a symbol of Christmas.

HOLLY

Ilex aquifolium
Holly family
Up to 15m
Evergreen

This bushy evergreen tree has smooth, silver~grey bark and shiny leaves which are also very spiky . . . OUCH!

Birds eat holly berries in winter when food is scarce.
WARNING:
They are poisonous to people.

Male and female flowers grow on separate trees. The female ones smell nice. Mind you don't prick your nose!

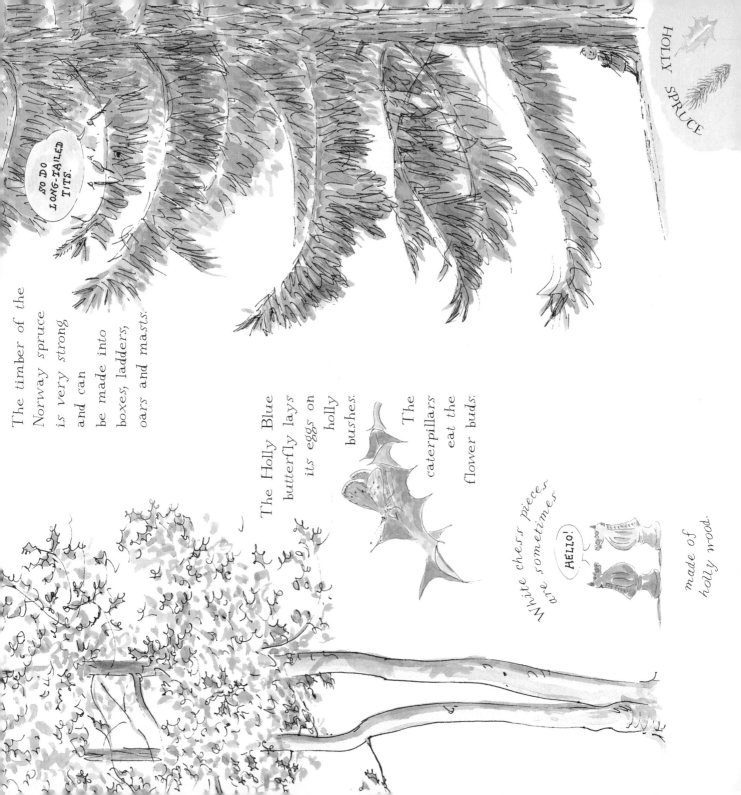

SO DO LONG-TAILED TITS.

The timber of the Norway spruce is very strong and can be made into boxes, ladders, oars and masts.

The Holly Blue butterfly lays its eggs on holly bushes.

The caterpillars eat the flower buds.

White chess pieces are sometimes

HELLO!

made of holly wood.

YEW

Taxus baccata
Yew family
Up to 25m
Evergreen

The yew is a grand, handsome tree, covered with reddish bark. Often found in churchyards, some are over 1,000 years old.

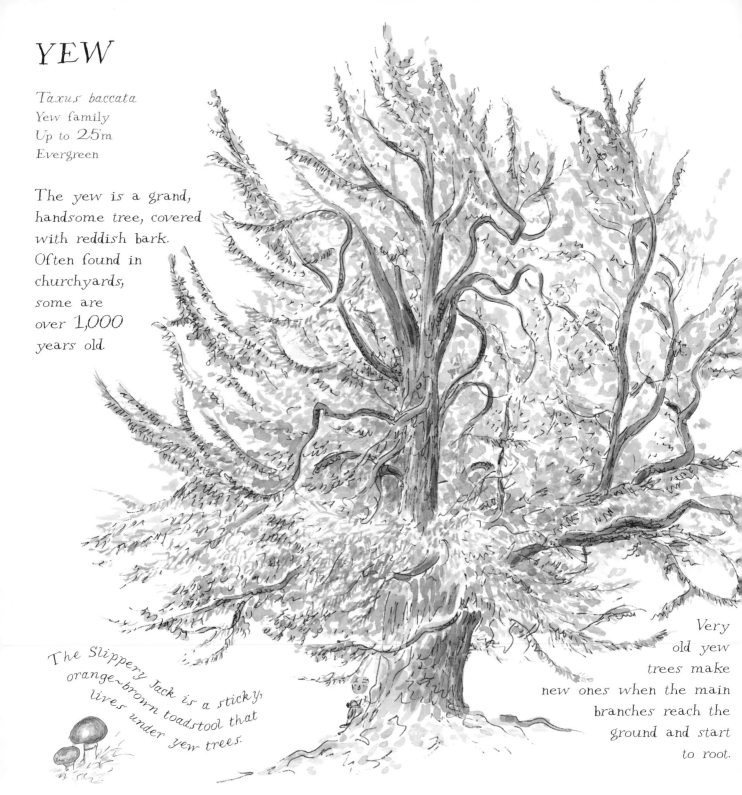

The Slippery Jack is a sticky, orange-brown toadstool that lives under yew trees.

Very old yew trees make new ones when the main branches reach the ground and start to root.

IN SPRING

Clouds of yellow pollen are released when you tap the male trees.

Legend says that Robin Hood used a bow made of yew.

IN AUTUMN

Look out for bright red fruits on the female trees. These are sometimes called 'snotty gogs' or 'snottle berries'.

BE CAREFUL! The seeds, leaves and bark of yew trees are very poisonous to people and most animals ~ except rabbits and deer.

Yews are covered with tiny, soft, flat, needle~like leaves.

Yew trees can be planted as hedges, made into mazes or cut into interesting shapes ~ this is called topiary.

55

DOUGLAS FIR

Pseudotsuga menziesii
Pine family
Up to 60m
Evergreen

This tall and slender tree comes originally from North America. Its grey~green smooth bark has sticky, scented blisters. The bark goes reddish brown as the tree gets older. The Douglas fir has needle~like leaves all year round.

In the past this fir's tall, straight trunk meant it was perfect for masts on sailing ships.

Legend says that the scales are shaped like tiny mice that once hid in the cones during forest fires.

DOUGLAS FIR

If you see
a slice of a cut tree,
you can tell its age
by counting the rings.
The rings of a
Douglas fir are very
clear and easy
to count.

The tree is named after
the nineteenth century
Scottish botanist David Douglas.
He was a brave explorer who
faced many dangers. His camp was
attacked by wild bears during his 10,000-mile trek
across America.

IN SPRING

Look out for the small
male flowers along
the branches,
under the
shoots, and
the female
flowers, which
look like little
shaving brushes,
at the tips.

OLIVE

Olea europaea
Olive family
Up to 15m
Evergreen

The olive branch is an international symbol of peace.

Olive trees grow in warm Mediterranean regions. They have long, leathery grey~green leaves. Olive fruits ripen from green to black. Their smooth grey bark goes all wrinkly in old age.

In ancient Greece a crown of olive leaves was given to a winner, whether in games or war.

ITALIAN CYPRESS

Cupressus sempervirens
Cypress family
Up to 23m
Evergreen

These beautiful tall, slender trees are a real feature of the Mediterranean. Their green columns can be seen poking up across the hillsides and gardens.

The leaves are tiny, evergreen and look like scales. The little cones can stay on the tree for years.

THE LEAVES ARE NOT SCENTED BUT THE TIMBER IS! MMM! SMELLS LOVELY!

In the Middle Ages it was used to make chests for clothes as the scented wood kept them smelling sweet!

59

The doors of St Peter's Basilica in Vatican City, Rome, are made from cypress wood.

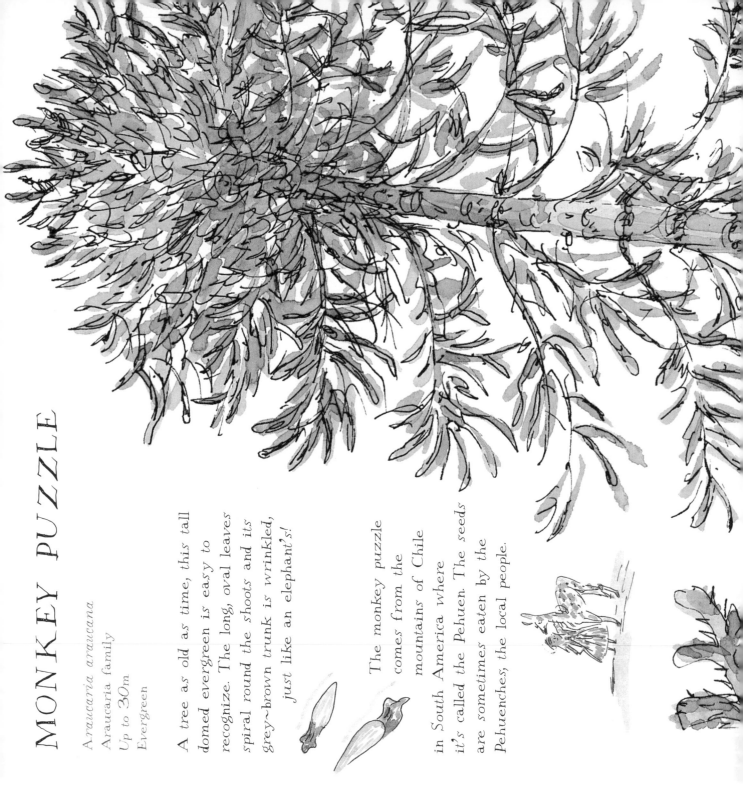

MONKEY PUZZLE

Araucaria araucana
Araucaria family
Up to 30m
Evergreen

A tree as old as time, this tall domed evergreen is easy to recognize. The long, oval leaves spiral round the shoots and its grey-brown trunk is wrinkled, just like an elephant's!

The monkey puzzle comes from the mountains of Chile in South America where it's called the Pehuen. The seeds are sometimes eaten by the Pehuenches, the local people.

MONKEY PUZZLE

It takes two years to grow a ring of new branches, but each tree can live for 1,000 years.

Its bark is heat-resistant so it often grows on the slopes of volcanoes.

The spiky leaves are almost triangular in shape and are thick and leathery. You will find male and female flowers growing on different trees.

Seeds brought to the UK by the plant hunters found their way into many Victorian gardens.

One owner remarked, 'It would puzzle a monkey to climb that', and the name monkey puzzle has stuck ever since.

The monkey puzzle was around 200 million years ago when dinosaurs ruled the Earth.

INDEX

TICK LIST

Tick off the trees as you find them.

- ☐ Alder
- ☐ Apple
- ☐ Apricot
- ☐ Ash
- ☐ Beech
- ☐ Blackthorn
- ☐ Cedar of Lebanon
- ☐ Cherry
- ☐ Common larch
- ☐ Dog rose
- ☐ Douglas fir
- ☐ Elder
- ☐ Field maple
- ☐ Hawthorn
- ☐ Hazel
- ☐ Holly
- ☐ Hornbeam
- ☐ Horse chestnut

- ☐ Italian cypress
- ☐ Lime
- ☐ Lombardy poplar
- ☐ London plane
- ☐ Monkey puzzle
- ☐ Norway spruce
- ☐ Oak
- ☐ Olive
- ☐ Plum
- ☐ Pear
- ☐ Rowan (mountain ash)
- ☐ Scots pine
- ☐ Silver birch
- ☐ Sweet chestnut
- ☐ Sycamore
- ☐ Willow
- ☐ Wych elm
- ☐ Yew

The Eden Project brings plants and people together.
It is dedicated to developing a greater understanding
of our shared global garden, encouraging us to
respect plants ～ and to protect them.

MY TREE SCRAPBOOK

These are your own pages for keeping a record of the
trees you see and the places in which you find them.

This book will help you to identify the trees that you find,
perhaps on holiday or just at home throughout the year. You can use
the following pages to list them, draw or paint them, or even stick in photos,
but ONLY pick and press leaves or flowers if they grow in your own garden.
The headings are suggestions only: use the space as you wish and
let your imagination run wild. Make sure you date all your
entries ~ this could be a useful document one day!

Enjoy mixing your colours to match the leaves, flowers and fruits
exactly and don't forget to include some of the insects
and birds you might see nearby.

This is your space. Fill it with trees!

TREES IN SPRING

LOMBARDY POPLAR April 1s

BEECH April 12th: In the park. The big beech tree has such soft new leaves.

HAZEL April 24.

All along the road side. The bright red catkins were blowing in the breeze.

PLUM March 15th: In next door's garden. The little flowers are so pretty.

n a hedge. Lots of dangly catkins ～ just like lambs' tails!

TREES IN SUMMER

CHERRY June 30th: Bottom of our garden. The tree's first fruit tasted amazing.

SYCAMORE June 1st: Granny's garden. There were so many bee

FIELD MAPLE July 2nd: On my afternoo

...llecting nectar from the flowers.

LONDON PLANE June 19th: All along our street. The prickly fruits look just like they do in the book!

...valk. I felt some of their soft, leathery leaves!

TREES IN AUTUMN

HORSE CHESTNUT October 10th: I found a HUGE conker in the park.

OAK September 10th: In the playing field. I picked up an acorn to plant in a pot.

LARCH October 1st: The

HAWTHORN September 20th: In the hedge. I saw a thrush eating the red haws!

Leaves on the larch in the forest were golden yellow.

TREES IN WINTER

LIME January 31st: On a school trip

SYCAMORE February 14th: Walking in the woods. I saw the crooked branches.

SWEET CHESTNUT January 10th: Grandpa's garden. I ran m

could tell by the whiskers and elbow~shaped branches.

hand across the trunk's spiral ridges.

HOLLY December 11th: We collected holly sprigs to decorate our front room.

FAVOURITE TREES

YEW October 25th: Under the churchyard yew. I saw a cluster of Slippery Jacks!

WILLOW July 19th: On the river. We rowed

CEDAR OF LEBANON August 10th: On holiday in Greece. We sheltered

...nder a huge willow. It was magical floating under the leaves.

...from the midday sun under the huge boughs.

DOG ROSE June 25th: I love the pale pink flowers.

TREES ON HOLIDAY

MONKEY PUZZLE

YEW

LOMBARDY POPLAR

COMMON LARCH

ITALIAN
CYPRESS

CEDAR OF LEBANON

OLIVE

SCOTS PINE

On a walk, I spotted a seed on the ground. I took it home and planted it in a pot.

A TREE OF
MY OWN

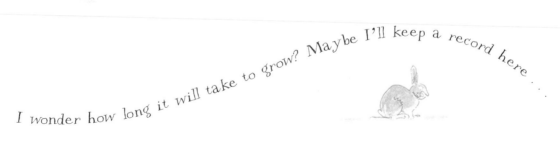

I wonder how long it will take to grow? Maybe I'll keep a record here . . .

At the bottom of the playing field there's a very large tree.

THE BIGGEST TREE
I EVER SAW

I measured it with my friend.

It was................tall, and it looked a bit like this.

For Kate

A LITTLE GUIDE TO TREES
AN EDEN PROJECT BOOK 978 1 903 91982 8

Published in Great Britain by Eden Project Books, an imprint of Transworld Publishers
A Random House Group Company

This edition published 2011

7 9 10 8 6

Text copyright © Kate Petty and Jo Elworthy, 2009
Illustrations copyright © Charlotte Voake, 2009

The right of Kate Petty, Jo Elworthy and Charlotte Voake to be identified as the authors
and illustrator of this work has been asserted in accordance with the Copyrights, Designs and Patents Act 1988.

Designed by Ness Wood

TRANSWORLD PUBLISHERS 61-63 Uxbridge Road, London, W5 5SA

www.edenproject.com   www.randomhousechildrens.co.uk

Addresses for companies within The Random House Group Limited can be found at: www.randomhouse.co.uk/offices.htm
THE RANDOM HOUSE GROUP Limited Reg. No. 954009

A CIP record for this book is available from the British Library.

The Eden Project is owned by the Eden Trust, a registered charity. Eden Project, Bodelva, St Austell, Cornwall PL24 2SG

Printed and bound in China